BURNED
BEYOND
RECOGNITION

*Has rejection caused you
to forget who you are?*

AUTHORED BY
LINDA JO KELLER

CONTRIBUTIONS BY
GREGORY R. KELLER

ISBN: 0615814050

ISBN 13: 9780615814056

Library of Congress Control Number: TXu 1-869-982

LCCN Imprint Name: New Berlin, WI

TABLE OF CONTENTS

ACKNOWLEDGEMENT

This project began in 2009 and was finally completed in 2014. Why did it take so long? When you happen to be someone with very little patience and a history of procrastination, the reason might make sense.

With the passing of my father and our move from Pennsylvania to Wisconsin; not to mention a few other distractions here and there, it just took a little longer than expected.

It was my loving husband who not only encouraged me to continue but constantly reminded me of my unfinished "bucket list". Although his repeated nudging was an annoyance, I am so thankful he never stopped.

Secondly, I must thank my sister. I asked her to look at it with an unbiased opinion. After reading it she responded with "I know you and you held back". She couldn't have been more correct. There were some stories about my past that I felt might offend someone. After realizing that the entire motive for this book is to let the reader feel they are not alone in their despair and that there is a way out, I spent time adding to the story. Thank you for helping me to keep it real!

Most importantly, I thank God for introducing me to my Lord and Savior Jesus Christ and for giving me the Holy Spirit for direction.

INTRODUCTION

Let me begin by saying that I am not an expert on rejection, although I do have years of experience in the subject matter. So maybe that does make me somewhat of an authority.

That being said, this is not a cure-all for your depression. I am not a doctor, psychologist, psychiatrist, or medicine woman. I am someone just like you who has had more than my share of negative encounters. I have handled some situations correctly and, regrettably, a lot incorrectly.

Like everyone else who made mistakes in life, I had to pay the price for my actions. Whether right or wrong, it sometimes took years before I realized the difference. In that time, I've had to make the necessary changes in my attitude. The best lesson in life is to learn from your own mistakes. However, just because you recognize your faults and adjust your actions or change your personality, that does not exclude you from becoming someone different than who you should be.

I once met a young man who was burned quite badly over most of his body. I didn't know him before then, and I couldn't tell you what he originally looked like. However I can tell you now it didn't matter what he looked like on the outside because from the inside he was a very special person. This made me think about what it means to be burned beyond recognition. Does that always refer to the outside or can the inside of a person be just as unfamiliar when burned by damaging events?

I want to share what I believe many others have encountered in their lives—disappointment, frustration, and failures. A lot of these can be attributed to a lack of understanding as to why we can't or won't stand up for ourselves. What happened in our past that causes us to cringe with fear or to doubt our choices?

We sometimes need to look back in order to look ahead for better days. But once we get hold of the freedom needed to stand strong, we will never have a reason to look back at our destructive past again. This is where a lot of us get caught; we seem to be comfortable in feeling sorry for ourselves and consistently going back to what made us uncomfortable in the first place. We end up going around the mountain again and again without learning how to go in the right direction to move forward.

This book tells of how I became someone I could not recognize. It describes how I've dealt with the demons that caused me self-doubt and insecurity, and how I eventually escaped to become the person I was originally created to be.

CHAPTER 1

Are You Comfortable?

I love water! I absolutely, positively, can't get enough—love water. Not just drinking water. I'm talking about lakes, oceans, pools, hot tubs—anything that you can just lie back in, letting it surround you. You know the place that people say they go when needing to relieve the stress? My paradise, my happy place, is someplace in or around water. I could stay in a pool or the ocean for hours on end and never stop smiling.

I think it all started at conception. Mom said that I was a very strong-willed baby. The day before she went into labor, I did a flip and positioned myself feet first. The doctor looked down and saw a foot sticking out. They thought I was letting them know it was time. She said that was a stark indication of just how independent I would become. Actually, I have a much different version.

The doctor had to reach in to get me out because I had one foot against her rib and I was kicking him with the other. I wasn't ready at all. I was warm and comfortable. I had food whenever I needed it, slept as long as I wanted, and enjoyed the nice relaxing sound of the heartbeat.

And let's not forget—I was in something like water! Oh, how I miss those days... But like all good times, the fun ended with the cold reality that I was no longer comfortable. I can't tell you if I did a lot of screaming, but I'm sure I must have wanted to crawl back in.

The pink blanket they wrapped around me was going to have to do for the time being.

When I was just an infant, Mom said that the grass was her best babysitter. While hanging out laundry, she would place a small blanket on the lawn, and I would not move beyond its edges. According to her, I was afraid to venture off the secure blanket because I hated the feel of the grass under my hands and knees. She said that even as a toddler I would come running into the house, holding out my dirty hands for her to quickly wash, as if some foreign substance was eating away at my skin.

At the age of five, I was enrolled in kindergarten. When you look at my class picture, I'm grinning from ear to ear. You would have thought that I was born to be in school surrounded by my new classmates. After all, I was created to make friends and have fun. What better place to start than in kindergarten.

I remember that my very favorite part of the day was finger painting time. I could make anything I wanted, and what I made was a thing of beauty—dots, lines, circles, and swirls of color. And, of course, there was the occasional hand print that defined the artist. Stick people and houses with chimneys were most likely the only things anyone could recognize.

But what was amazing to me was that I absolutely loved the feel of the sticky, gooey paint squishing between my fingers. How could this be? Is this the same little girl who just a few years earlier was agonizing over the speck of dirt caught in the small crack of her hand? What spell did this paint and paper have over her? Could they have been the healing properties needed to overcome the fear of filth and grime?

Much later in life, I realized what made me change from prim and prissy to a Monet wannabe. It was my outlet, my analyst's couch, my stand-back-and-be-amazed. It didn't matter that my hands were dirty again. All that mattered was that I could be me, and without reservation. My imaginings had become real on paper. I had discovered creativity.

When we create, we're expressing who we really are. It doesn't make a difference if it comes from our hands, our voices, our instruments. We're showing the part of us that's most unusual—most different from others. This very thing, the ability to create, is often hidden and sometimes put away in the dark when we're rejected. I would soon find out how easily my youthful visions could be taken away.

First grade—wow! I'd finally graduated to the big time. Students from more advanced classes were walking around the same building as me. We were all wearing the same uniform. Sometimes we were permitted to share the same space outside when it was time for recess. I was excited again; there was a whole new group of people to get to know.

Although I was happy to discover new things, I was disappointed when I found out finger painting was no longer a requisite in the first grade. I guess I would have to survive on learning to write my name in block letters. That was so primitive considering that current first graders know how to play video games on laptops.

My boredom was soon interrupted by the teacher's announcement that we would have show-and-tell day. Now, that's what I'm talking about! Finally, the opportunity to once again express myself by showing all of my newfound friends what I was all about.

That morning, I decided to take my best friend and doll. The most amazing part about her—she could talk! Just pull her string and she would tell you her name. She was cute and fun. There couldn't have been a better doll made for me. She said all the right things and, just like me, made new friends easily.

I can still remember walking to school with her in my arms. I couldn't wait for all the class to meet her. We would pull her string together and then laugh and giggle at everything she had to say. All the girls would fall in love with her, and the boys would be jealous they didn't have something as fun to show and tell. I would be the talk of the town. This was going to be the best day ever.

As I strutted into the classroom, I soon took notice of the small groups beginning to form. There was a hush over the room, and eventually some snickering and pointing my way. I looked around me, thinking someone else must have walked in next to me. No chance. They were looking and laughing right at me. I had brought a *doll* to school. After all, first graders should be more mature than that, right?

I can't remember if I ever stood up front to show off my friend. However, I do remember holding on tight to her and crying all the way home. My dreams of self-expression and originality had been shattered.

This was my first experience that I can recall with the numbing pain of rejection. How could anyone not like her or, even more surprising, not like me? What would I have done if I had known they were going to react like that? Would I have taken something different to show? Maybe something that everyone would have liked? What compromise would I have made if it meant that I would have been accepted?

How does a young child deal with something like rejection? Some find it easier to handle if they withdraw from the crowd. Others find comfort in becoming just like everyone else. I did a little of both. There were days when I came out a little and tried to be a member of the group. Then there were days when I found it very difficult to get up in the morning and go to school. I wasn't the only one who went through rough patches growing up. There were others in my class who felt alone and not so easily accepted. There was always the overweight child, the skinny one, the one with glasses, the shy one, and the challenged one. Then there were the ones who rebelled from authority, and the class clowns who had to interrupt just to get attention.

My favorite escape from school was when we would visit my mother's parents. My grandfather was a quiet man, and from what I can remember, he seemed to keep to himself a lot. He would come home from work with his lunch pail in hand, and after taking off his work boots, he'd put them on the second step of the basement stairs and rotate the next set of boots to wear the next day.

He always had something for me when he came home. He'd reach into his shirt pocket and give me a coin or piece of candy. It didn't matter to me. I was just delighted to be around him. Sometimes he would get out the record player and play some old 45s. He'd play them over and over for me if I asked. One day he took me to his barber to get a haircut. Mom was furious when I came home with a short pixy cut. Again, it didn't matter to me. We were out having fun together.

He had a work area in the basement that was so intriguing to me that every time he went there I had to follow. I thought it was special that he would allow me to sit and watch him as he tinkered with his tools. There were bins and small boxes where he kept all his screws, wires, nuts, and bolts. I was amazed by the way he organized all his stuff. Everything had its place, and I'm sure that he would know instantly if something was missing or put away in the wrong bin.

After complaining of headaches, and having numerous tests, he ended up in the hospital. Mom took me for a visit, along with my two young brothers and my little baby sister. She'd just been born, and mom wanted him to see her. He took my hand, and we went for a walk down the hall from the visiting room. I knew something was wrong when he tried to read a sign and had the words all mixed up. He looked at my brothers and told them he was going to take them for a hair cut when he got out of there. Something inside told me that would never happen. He passed away just a few days later. I was so hurt that someone that special would leave me so quickly. How could I ever trust anyone to get that close to me again? I was going to miss our visits with him because home wasn't always the most secure place. My father was a very angry and violent man. Visiting my grandparents was a refuge for me.

I remember dreaming about my grandfather after his passing. I saw him wave to me from across the street where I was standing. It somehow made me feel as if he was still around. It just proves to me how there are certain people in your life that can make a deep impression, good or bad.

When I met my husband, I found out that he had lost his father the same year my grandfather passed away. My husband was only 16 years old at the time. His dad never saw him continue to play football or watch him go to state competition in gymnastics. He never knew that he became a carpenter just as he was or proudly wear his Navy uniform. He never met his grandchildren or great-grandchildren. However, in that short time that he was alive, he taught my husband how to become a disciplined young man.

In all the time I've known my husband, he has never looked back at his father's passing and complained or used it as an excuse to be angry or depressed. On the contrary, he became a stronger and more mature individual than any man I've known. He knows what it means to be respectful and how to complete any task that he sets his mind to accomplish. I have never seen him give up on anything. He is an example of what it means to move forward no matter what obstacle is put in his way.

CHAPTER 2

A Suitable Companion

D espite my early disappointments, my parents said that I grew up to be a very friendly child. They once lost me in a store in the mall because I was off making new friends. They soon found me tugging at a stranger's pants while looking up with a smile to announce, "Hi, my name's Linda." It was so important that everyone knew who I was, and I needed to know them as well. I was meeting the world one pant leg at a time. Although I was just an innocent child trying to have fun, there was an inherent need to be accepted. There is always a longing to feel good about oneself. This natural desire is not wrong. It's the way we go about finding attention that can be harmful.

I've always enjoyed meeting new people. However, I will admit to being a bit prejudiced. You see, I enjoy happy, upbeat people; I dislike angry, negative people. Because of that, I love and I hate people. I'm not confused, just being honest. Depending on the circumstances, there are many who would agree with me. It's not hard liking someone who's nice to you. Yet it's easy not wanting to be around someone who makes you feel uncomfortable. Maybe that's why so many have a tough time with relationships. It takes a lot of work to trust people enough to let them get close.

My encounter with mistrust started very early. As I mentioned before, our home life was not the type of place I would want any child to live through. It was like living on a fast moving roller coaster, but without being strapped in with the safety belt. The force of gravity kept us in place but I sometimes hoped it would slow down enough that I could jump off.

The one saving grace was my mother, who was and still is a very caring woman. I can remember as a young girl watching my mom cook and bake, hoping I could do as well. She worked tirelessly as a nurse on third shift. I never understood when she had time to sleep. Every morning she would come home from work and we would wake up to breakfast. Then at noon we came home to lunch, went back to school and returned again to a hot dinner. She spent time with us on homework and special projects.

She drove us to all of our school activities and still had time to go on school trips as a volunteer. There was never a time when we were young that I can recall her being ill. Ironically, it wasn't until after she retired from nursing that she caught the flu. She was too busy to get sick. It was when she stopped that the germs had a chance to catch up. Even after her nursing career ended, she still took care of her mother who lived alone and my father at home until they both passed away.

As a lot of teenage rebellious daughters, I never showed my mom the true respect that was due her. It was after I became an adult that I realized everything she sacrificed for her children. One thing that I know was especially hard for her was staying married to my father. Unfortunately, I believe it was because of us that she stayed. I don't blame her or hold her responsible for the suffering as children of an abusive father. If anything, I can say that I understand why women remain in sadistic relations. They hold on to the hope of change and sometimes live with the guilt of starting the relationship in the first place.

The one very disturbing part of having a violent father was that parents were quite fearful of allowing their child to become my friend. There was a time in grade school when some girls in my class stopped talking to me. I remember telling my mother that I didn't want to go to school anymore. It was too painful to stand in the shadows while the kids whispered about my family. Eventually the stigma of being different wore off and I made new friends. But those scars remain on a child for years.

Grade school can be rough. Kids at that age need to develop a sense of belonging. We want to fit in no matter the cost. Depending on your upbringing, you might be a leader or a follower. Children who were nurtured by their guardians have a tendency to know what they want, and they will blaze the path. Conversely, those who were ignored are disadvantaged and tag along just hoping to be noticed.

I understand that this is not always the case. There are some who push through a difficult childhood and make their own pathway. In either case, they all still have to cope with learning how to stand against the crowd.

Just as animals can sense the weak from the strong, we gravitate toward the more popular kids. We will try to act like them, talk like them, and even look like them. I was fortunate to attend a school that had uniforms. Other than hiking up our skirts to look older, there wasn't a lot you could do to stand out when it came to dress, although there were some girls who were allowed to wear makeup and earrings. I wore some makeup, much to my parent's dissatisfaction, but I didn't get my ears pierced until the age of eighteen.

One day, I was asked to go along with some girls to the mall. This was exciting for me because I didn't usually get asked to go places with them. When we finally arrived we spent time looking around at the latest clothing and accessories, all the while laughing and carrying on as young girls do. This was a great day for me. Suddenly, I was walking into a store, and when I turned around to talk to them, they ran away from me. I spent some time looking for them in the different stores but soon gave up. I remember standing there in the middle of crowds of people walking past me, and feeling like I was the only person in the entire building. I didn't understand what happened and why they did that to me. I walked home alone, crying and cold as it started to rain.

When something like that happens you have self-doubt and start questioning what is wrong with you that others won't accept. I began to look at myself in a different way and put on a negative image. This reflection would prove devastating in the future. It took me a long time before I believed anything I did was of value.

I found ways to transfer my frustrations to something more productive. In the fourth grade we were given the opportunity to learn an instrument, the piano or guitar. And since we didn't have a piano at home, the guitar was the obvious choice for me. My hands were very small and my family wasn't really sure I'd be able to wrap my fingers around the neck. I did just fine.

There was another girl in my class who had decided to take piano lessons. While the rest of the class went home for lunch, we would stay to eat our bagged lunch, then take our lessons with the music teacher. We each looked forward to seeing what the other brought for lunch. She was the first person to introduce me to Melba toast, and she played the piano as if it was second nature. I found out that she also practiced a lot at home. That's what made her so good. My teacher, however, had to write at the top of my lesson book, "Linda must practice at least forty-five minutes per day in order to perfect the assigned material." I still have that book and note just to remind me that nothing you want comes easy.

Music was something that both my parents enjoyed. My dad played the drums in school and later in a jazz band. He also sang with the church choir, both as a child and an adult. Mom didn't sing or play, although she would have loved to learn the piano. But she did introduce me to all types of music very early in my life. We would put on the old 45s or LPs and listen to everything from classical to the latest hits. I would sit on the floor in front of the stereo and sing along to every song—making up the words, of course.

Music was going to become my new creative outlet. Although finger painting was still my old favorite, it was time for something new. There I was at the age of nine expressing myself with chords and notes like nobody's business. My teacher was in charge of the annual school recital and asked if I wanted to play a duet, with her on the piano and me on guitar. The audience stood to applaud when we were finished. I was automatically hooked and soon I decided it was time to take the show on the road.

I wanted a band of my own and I knew the only way to start one was to first write original pieces. I soon went to work and started creating my very first song. It had something to do with a clown and that's all I remember. Linda and the Christian Zippers were coming to a stage near you. Don't ask me where I came up with that name, but I have it in writing from the time when I asked my parents to let me have a concert at school using that stage name. We did play at school, but only for a few teachers and a small number of friends. The big times were going to have to wait until much later.

I continued my lessons, playing guitar at church, and was paid once for a neighborhood kid's birthday party. I took a few classical lessons. I even tried the electric guitar with a loud, booming amplifier. That didn't last long. It wasn't mom and dad's taste. I even had the opportunity to play and sing with my teacher for an annual telethon. It was on one of the local television stations, and one of my classmates accidentally saw it.

For me, music is a familiar and faithful friend. When I'm down, I can always depend on feeling better after playing something on the guitar, or just listening to a song.

But that dear companion would soon be replaced. I was finding a new and more exciting hobby—boys!

Have you ever found yourself standing with the refrigerator door open and looking in to find something that you just know you need, but you're not even sure what it is or whether or not you should have it? You close the door once, maybe twice, but keep reopening it hoping that mystery item will finally appear. You'll instantly know that it was exactly what you were looking for all along. That's how it is when you're a teenager.

You look at the boys in your class with some sort of wanting, but you're not really sure you understand what it is that you want. Desire is a funny thing. It can be the best feeling and the worst feeling you've ever had. Once you find yourself attached to someone, you realize that it just doesn't feel like you thought it would, and you soon become so terribly disappointed.

We called it "going with" someone. My dad would frustrate me when he'd hear that expression and ask me, "Where are you going?" I couldn't answer him with anything but, "You just don't understand!" And, well, quite honestly neither did I. And when it was all over—the "going with" part—he "broke up" with you. Funny that we used those words to describe no longer having a boyfriend, because sometimes it actually felt like someone broke me. That was a sad thought that yesterday you were accepted, but today you're set aside and replaced by another girl.

Looking back, I admire the girls who didn't have the same need to have a boyfriend. They spent their time studying or being with family. Not me. I was a boy crazed junky, and I didn't feel complete if I couldn't write some boy's name on my books. There was an empty hole inside of me when I didn't have a boyfriend. We didn't actually do anything. We would just hang out together and sometimes hold hands. It was enough knowing that I was needed and wanted by someone else. That feeling would eventually turn into an obsession.

CHAPTER 3

Lost and Found

Moving out of the eighth grade, where you're comfortable and know all your classmates, and then into high school with strangers was both exhilarating and frightening. We were the "big cheese" back there. Now we're the little freshman.

Mom made me an outfit for my first day. Maxi dresses were in style at the time, and she created a beautiful light denim jumper with a white long sleeve blouse that I wore with a pair of black patent leather shoes. I can still remember trying to walk like I had kept some of the authority from the last school. I tried to blend in with the upper classmen as I entered at the front door of the high school. I then noticed someone point to me and say, "There's a freshman." Was I really that obvious?

My earlier fears of fitting in were soon dispelled by the fact that all of us were new at this. Soon it became apparent that there were different cliques that would eventually group together. Some were drawn to the academic, some to the athletic, and some to the artistic. We found our familiar pairings and eventually grew apart from the class that we were once so close to.

Later, as adults, we came together again for a grade school class reunion. It was the best reunion I had ever attended. We reminisced about the old teachers, friends, family, and fun times that were never forgotten—no matter how much time and how many people had separated us over the many, many years. There seems to be something about young children who are growing and experiencing life together. There is a unique bond that's created. We were all growing and learning about our future at the same time.

High school presented some very interesting possibilities. There were a lot more activities to become involved in. Even though I was a cheerleader in grade school, it was very apparent that I didn't hold a candle to the girls from the other schools. I tried out and failed miserably. I soon moved on to trying out for the marching band. My mom was a flag majorette in the same school, and maybe I had some of the same skills. Not an ice cube's chance in… Well, not in that school. I once again failed.

My siblings were, and still are, great athletes, so what about me? I couldn't dribble a basketball to save my life, but I thought I might be good at softball. I was cut after the first tryout. Now what? There was always music. I was involved in the chorus, and once played the guitar for a school assembly. Looking back, I could have been involved in so much more. There was drama, debate team, school politics, and anything else that would have kept me in line.

I was more interested in socializing outside of school. Remember how curiosity killed the cat? Well I was more than curious. I was dangerously inquisitive about anything that involved rebellion. I can still remember the very first time I was introduced to pot. A friend and I were walking home from a dance when two boys from another school approached us. They asked if we wanted to try it. Remember, up to this point I had no fear, was very curious, and liked boys. How could I say no? What would they think of me if I said no?

There I was—a teenager with prior experience in peer rejection. I certainly didn't want to look scared, and that was a great opportunity to be labeled "cool." I had already started smoking cigarettes, so why not pot? After that day, anything and everything that presented itself as a way to defy the rules was okay by me. Somehow this change of behavior was a way of expressing myself without having to worry about being separated from all the others.

Drug and alcohol use was widely accepted among our age group. It was the 70s era and parties were everywhere. It was a good way to once again meet new people—one of my favorite pastimes.

Reading this you may feel that I'm being too casual about making the wrong decisions. That is not my intention. I want you to understand why young people do what they do. It's not always because they're bad children and you're a terrible parent. It could be because they lack the mental discipline it takes to do the right thing. We're programmed early in life, and any emotional chaos can often block the mind from wanting to do what is right. It becomes all about feeling good and not having to deal with the bad.

My drug use started with trying to impress someone by smoking pot. Soon it was easy for me to do whatever was available. Cocaine, LSD, Hash and Opium were attractive and not at all scary. It was a way to escape the trauma and avoid the memories. Although that was the way I handled things, I would never recommend that anyone follow my lead. There is a great price to pay both emotionally and physically when you abuse your body.

So just how big is the physical world of a teenager? Let's think about that. A baby's world consists of the crib it sleeps in and its mother's arms—not very big, but I don't think they do much complaining. What about a preteen or teenager? It most likely will include a friend's house, the classroom, ball field, and—if you're a girl—the mall!

But the emotional world is a completely different place. It's a whole lot bigger than what we can imagine. Dealing with peer pressure involves every aspect of life. How do I look? How do I sound? What do I wear? What should I say? Am I smart enough, pretty enough, talented enough to fit in? What will they think of me? We should teach our children to first love themselves, then they won't be so concerned about what others think.

I can remember back when I was in school there were few incidents where students were bullied. But never in my years have I noticed so many acts of torment as I see on the news. It looks to me as if there are a large number of angry youth. We need to reach out to our children more now than ever before.

If you see your child moving in the direction of self-destruction, whether that might be mood changes, isolation, eating disorders, or emotional outbreaks, you may want to consider sitting them down and asking a very simple question. How do you feel about yourself?

I realize that most young people are not going to want to sit and discuss their feelings with an adult, especially their own parent. But what if that very simple question opens up a door to begin the healing process?

If you go back to those days, try to remember what was important to you. What makes sense to you now as an adult meant little or nothing then. We didn't worry about the future as much. We lived in the now. The reasons behind our actions were clear as mud to us, but we didn't stop to think about how it might affect us later in life. We were influenced by sight, not thought.

However insignificant you might believe your teenager's stress is to you, it's a big deal to them. If they're making mountains out of molehills, help them get to the top. Watch and listen. Respect them. *You may not live in their world, but you can be a great ambassador when visiting.*

When I was a teenager, I didn't feel comfortable talking to my parents about my issues. It's not that mom wouldn't listen to me; she was busy caring for my younger siblings and had enough problems of her own to deal with. My dad was not the consoling type and I was too afraid of him to share my deepest secrets. I kept a lot of my troubles to myself and looked to drugs and alcohol to try to forget them.

My dad had been abused as a child. He started out his life rejected by his parents when they gave him over to his paternal grandmother. The stories about her were frightening. Apparently, she had a speakeasy back in the prohibition days and ran a prostitution house where my father was raised. He said that she would have him dance and sing for her clients and "pass around the hat" for expenses. If he didn't comply, she would beat him and send him to bed without dinner.

When he had the chance, he ran away and lived among homeless men who taught him how to stuff newspapers in his clothing to stay warm. He once spent time in jail after getting caught during an armed robbery. Although there was no excuse for him to become the angry man that he was later in life, I can understand what caused him to be that way.

He mirrored his upbringing by acting out in rage when things didn't go his way. We were all on the receiving end of numerous whippings with his belt. Dad didn't show restraint when he was upset. I felt sorry for my brothers and sister when they were involved in sports. Dad would yell and embarrass them if they didn't do well. Is it any wonder why we are all so competitive and hate to lose?

Mom had no idea he was like that when they met. He had a way of appealing to the ladies and she was no different. She said she was captivated by his blue eyes and he was a great dancer.

I always thought that I was too smart to ever get involved with someone that would hurt me. But when you are only looking at the physical and not the emotional, you can miss a lot. There was a boy in my class that I couldn't stop thinking about. He was attractive enough to get the attention of many girls. Right there was my problem, he was a challenge. If I could win the interest of a popular guy, maybe I would get the respect I wanted. We started dating and I found myself caught up in those big blue eyes and never saw what was coming.

One night we went to a concert. A friend of his drove us and we stopped to get some bottles of wine for on the way. The concert was a blur due to the fact that I was high, drunk and stupid! On the way home, we sat in the back together. He started to kiss me and I pushed him away because I was feeling sick. His desire was stronger than I was. After punching and grabbing my hands and legs, he forced himself on me. The only thing I could do was scream for the driver to stop and let me out of the car.

When I got home, I was bruised, bleeding and now a victim of date rape.

I was no longer a virgin and didn't experience my first time in the romantic way that I had fantasized about as a young girl. Although he was the aggressor, I now recognize that I was also at fault for letting it happen. I'm not saying that every woman is responsible for a man taking advantage of her like that.

But why would I put myself in such a dangerous position? The answer is that it was a game for me and although I considered myself the victor, I lost big time! After that, I saw sex as a weapon and not something beautiful with my future husband. I used being seductive as a tool to hurt and control any man that thought I was weak. No one was going to have that kind of power over me again.

After watching my mom go through so much with my dad, I can't thank God enough for the man I married. Not only is he my best friend, but he is someone that never takes me for granted. I can trust him with my heart and he makes me feel special even when I'm not so wonderful.

CHAPTER 4

What Do You Really See?

W e have a tendency to want change in our lives by altering the outside in order to define the inside. But we have it backward. What we need to do is first transform the inside, and then we'll change how we see the outside, both in ourselves and in others. We want to believe that how we look defines who we are. When in reality, who we are on the inside is how people should see us on the outside. Let me give you a few examples.

When someone does a random act of kindness for you, do you really notice the color of their eyes, the texture of their hair, or what clothing they're wearing? Maybe you do if you're a profiler or just naturally nosey. Better yet, do you really think that when you stop and let someone go in front of you at the grocery store, she goes home and says to her family, "A guy with brown eyes, wavy brown hair, and wearing a blue jacket let me go in front of him when I was in a hurry"? Most likely the only thing she says is that someone was kind to her. That's enough for her to remember you.

Or what about how we automatically put labels on people depending on what they're wearing or have on their bodies. There was a time in my life when I would literally judge an individual for having tattoos, or rings in there face. I didn't get it—until I saw someone who from the outside you would have thought just recently escaped from prison, but who was actually a mentor for young adults. The kids could relate better to him than to a stuffy, well-dressed minister. It became a matter of trust and relationship rather than looks.

I now have three tattoos of my own. One is a multi-colored musical staff on the left side of my chest. I write songs and it represents colorful music coming from my heart. The other two are special to me and stand for what I believe. I get it now!

Why is it that whenever we look at ourselves in the mirror we believe that what we see is the same as what everyone else is seeing. I haven't found that to be true. Try this one day. Stand in front of your mirror, and just smile at yourself. How do you feel? Okay, silly, but what do you see? I can tell you that what you're looking at is not always what other people see, especially when you're doing something nice for them. They're not noticing the flaws that you happen to pick out every time you're looking in the mirror.

There are times that I see myself completely different from one day to the next depending on how I feel. So now, how do you change something as radical as the way you see yourself? It starts with a little bit of faith and a lot of humility. It starts with admitting that you don't know how to love yourself. You've never been told that it's even possible. It also begins by *changing your confession* about yourself. The words you say when talking about how you feel can be either self-destructive or self-improving.

Let's begin with a few simple questions. Have you made wrong decisions in your life? Do you know others that have made wrong decisions? How do you see them? Do you view them as ugly and wicked as you see yourself? Are you so much harder on you when considering the verdict? What are you willing to do to change? Self-examination can be very difficult. Don't give up so easily when considering your past.

We're born into a challenging world. From the first breath, we begin screaming for comfort. Babies aren't crying from the womb just to test their lung capacity. They're looking for anyone readily available to make them feel safe, secure. That is no different than what you're experiencing now as an adult. You still need to feel safe and secure. Lately I've noticed from the people I encounter day-to-day that uncertainty seems to be the norm. Security, self-expression, individuality should be the norm. How is it that we say we want to be accepted, when we can't even accept ourselves?

I was surprised when I found out that the simple ant can actually lift almost five thousand times its own weight. Without thought, without trepidation, without even thinking about how it feels that day, that little ant actually lifts something that is so much bigger than itself. What about the huge two-ton elephant that can gingerly walk around its much smaller baby. Without worry, without first looking into the mirror and complaining about how big it is, it automatically considers the delicacy of its steps. It would be great if we reacted to situations based on simple conviction rather than having to think about what affect it will have on us.

Rejection is not just when someone doesn't accept us in their club or when we are turned down for a job. Rejection is also when someone is unkind to us or unfriendly in a way that makes us feel bad. We naturally want to be loved and anything opposite of that hurts.

We feel rejected when we're not recognized, whether for our physical attributes, talents, or skills. But we live in an atmosphere where everything we see formulates how we feel. We're surrounded by unreasonable media. Advertising gives us the idea that we will never be good enough until we conform. We have to realize that commercials, magazines, and stores have paid marketing firms. They purposely use the beautiful and famous to sell. That is not reality. That is not you. You can buy what they're trying to sell. But no matter what it is, it will never make you into someone different. Just broke and a lot more frustrated.

I grew up in a very competitive family. And although I wasn't the athletic type, I still found myself wanting to be good at anything I tried. Growing up in that atmosphere I found myself becoming angry when things didn't go my way. I believe that this attitude caused me to become frustrated when I couldn't control my environment. Anger was an emotion that I felt most comfortable in expressing. How do we react when we can't control our environment? How do we process our thoughts? In my opinion, this is where we lose ourselves. When we try to alter our circumstances, we change the very matrix of who we really are. I admire people who can stand up for anything they believe without compromise.

I have been in situations where I needed to take a hard position—to decide between speaking the truth and agreeing with a lie. Honestly I can say I didn't always do the right thing because of fear. Fear of not saying what was expected or fear of looking foolish.

When I didn't stand up, I paid a price. Yet, when I did do the right thing, I also paid a price. Which way seems to be more difficult? Do you suffer for what's right, or do you suffer for what's wrong? Pay now or pay later?

How many times have we heard it said that everyone tells a little white lie now and then? How far does deception go before it becomes okay? Although you can lie to others, you can never lie to yourself or God. The truth will always be there to remind you of your dishonesty. However, honesty is the key. The key to your repentance and repentance is the key to your salvation. Salvation will cause you to eventually become a trustworthy person.

But it takes a lot of humility to admit that you have faults. You might say that sometimes you're not nice to people or that there are times when you're impatient. That's not exactly what I mean. I'm talking about admitting that you think and do things that no one else sees. You might think that lusting after someone else's spouse is okay as long as no one else knows. You might think that lying to someone about the simplest of matters is okay as long as no one else knows. How much more do you think will eventually be okay as long as no one else knows?

If you are uncomfortable when you tell a lie, that's a good sign. If you don't think twice about being deceptive, you should worry. Deception is tricky. It can hide behind a mask of compromise and make it seem that it's okay as long as no one gets hurt. Don't be fooled. Every lie, deception, con or fraud is eventually exposed. How do you think the media gets their stories? Someone always comes forward with the truth. Think twice before entering into a secret bond. Whether it's gossip about someone in the office or cheating on your spouse, someone always gets hurt.

You may be wondering what all this has to do with rejection. We must first learn how to search deep in our souls in order to find out what trigger points cause us the most pain.

Look at all the murder and suicide by individuals you would never have thought capable of it. They move into a realm of darkness that causes them to lose sight of their own value. The lines cross between right and wrong, and soon it's difficult to distinguish what the conscience is trying to say. How long do you think it would take before your mind would trick you into believing it would be okay to take another life, or even your own?

I believe when people experience a lot of rejection and don't know how to become free, they become easily deceived. Rejection is the oldest form of deception. It tells lies about yourself or others. Gossip is a subtle form of rejection. You might think it's okay because the person you're talking about doesn't know. You're still projecting a negative image on that individual.

Unfortunately, I've encountered this in prayer groups. We think that we're "sharing" about someone so that the group will have knowledge of what to pray about. This is not always the case. We need to first consider what we discuss. Someone in the group may have an issue with the person we're talking about, and we just gave them more fuel for the fire.

I have a problem with those who feel it's their mission in life to tell others what's wrong with them. Why would you want to tell another person that they're insecure? Doesn't that just add to their inability to feel safe when you point out their faults? What is it about your own past that makes you feel superior enough to reveal another's imperfections?

I'm not referring to when someone is in counseling and asks for help in those areas. But even in that circumstance, a counselor needs to be careful about how far to go with reprimanding the patient. Even if the individual has a pattern of getting easily offended, they should still be given the respect of gentle reproach.

I have been on both ends. I have found that religious counselors can often be the most dangerous when it comes to giving advice. We sometimes hide behind the bible and use it as a weapon. If you want to help others by preaching, teaching, or counseling, first be sure to live what you share. You're often tested in those same areas, and if you have only head knowledge and not actual life experience, you'll find yourself in trouble. I have lost a number of old friends from living in the Christian bubble of self-righteousness. After all these years, I want nothing more than to be able to take back the things I said that caused them to no longer want my friendship.

If you want to be Christ-like, then read how He lived in absolute humility. That doesn't mean He was weak. On the contrary, it takes more strength to do what's right than to follow the crowd. He was so careful in what He said and how He said it. He knew His purpose on this earth.

I've always been astounded by the fact that Jesus Christ was God in the flesh with the power to change what caused Him pain, and yet He only did what He knew His Father wanted Him to do. There was a time when He asked if there was another way than to endure what He knew would be extreme agony. Yet, He learned obedience by the things that He suffered. I'm not saying we need to hang on a cross, but we do need to die to ourselves before wanting to change the world.

CHAPTER 5

Sticks and Stones

I have wanted to write a book since I was a young girl. I remember thinking that I would name it *Hindsight*. The problem was that I wasn't old enough to have enough hindsight to talk about. I just wanted to write about people and how we relate to one another. Even as a child I was acutely aware of relationships and how people would act depending on the individual. It seemed they would treat the child that was well off and appealing with a tender voice. Yet the poor and unattractive child would receive a harsher response to the same situation.

I once had a teacher call me into her office to discuss my after school activities. There were a number of us that would hang out together close to the school grounds until dark. Nothing illegal or dangerous took place, although some of us did smoke cigarettes. She began to accuse me of using drugs and alcohol and said that she had a few of my classmates watching me.

At the time, there was nothing true about her accusation. But for whatever reason, she believed I was trouble. Ironically the ones she had spying on me were some of my friends that were also out late at night. Her perception of me was tainted and I became a target of ridicule. Her claim made me angry and frustrated.

Was she just trying to warn me or did she really believe what she said? Either way, it was in her approach that changed my attitude. Nothing about her words were caring or concerning. She was critical and I left that meeting feeling rejected and insecure.

Rather than proving her wrong, I made up my mind to rebel against authority. If I was going to be accused of wrong doing, I might as well do wrong. I'm aware it was the complete opposite of what I should have done. But I was going to defend my territory and no one was going to point the finger at me again. Unfortunately, her falsehood of me eventually became fact. I don't blame her for my rebellion but I do blame her for the way she handled the problem.

If we are going to point children in the right direction, then we should learn how to use our words. Yes, there are times that call for a strong reprimand. However, making accusations out of flawed thinking can cause a child to take the wrong path. Watch how and what you say. Consider your objective with kind words that will show the child your concern. Remember, you can catch more flies with honey than vinegar.

I'm astonished by people who have physical challenges—whether brought on at birth, an accident, or by an act of terror—who still have more self-confidence than I did. How is it that they find encouragement and strength rather than digging a hole of depression? When I see this I have to ask myself who I really want to be. Should I be someone who finds fault in everything I do, or someone who looks past myself and considers the needs of others?

If we stay bound within our own parameters, then we miss the opportunity to help someone else. If everyone would think outside the box and reach past their comfort zone, maybe there wouldn't be so much anger and frustration in the world.

I'm not talking about giving all your money away or selling all your goods in order to help the poor. A simple gesture or smile can make the difference in someone's day. I look for opportunities to do something nice for someone else. I don't do it for accolades or to receive something in return. I do it because it feels good, and because, hopefully, that person will feel good enough to do something for someone else. I know this isn't a new concept. However I do believe it doesn't happen as often as it should.

Years ago our church started a clothing drive. About a dozen or more gathered slightly used clothing, and we hung it up in the downstairs of our church. We put an ad in the local paper announcing free clothing for one day. This idea grew to where we had to have it outside in a park. Hundreds of people came with bags and boxes to load up for their family. A number of people asked me, "What about those people who get a lot of clothing and take it home to sell?" My response was that for all I knew, anyone who came needed the clothing, and it was given freely without restrictions. What they did with it after they left was between them and God. We shouldn't think about the consequences when giving, just give.

It's that simple. How do you know that one small gesture wouldn't cause them to feel positive about the world around them? Something as simple as opening a door for someone or offering to buy a meal can make the biggest difference in that life. How many times have you thought about calling someone, and when you did, you found out they needed to talk. We have an inner voice that's always telling us about the needs of others. But what if we have that voice turned off because we're too self-involved?

There will always be opportunities to help. We just need to listen and look without prejudice. There may come a time when you're the one with the need. If you don't know how to sow, then what is it you'll eventually reap? A farmer can't look forward to gathering large crops if he never planted any seeds.

Recently I read a story about unusual animal friendships, like the cat that has a pet rat, or the Bengal tiger cub that hangs out with a chimpanzee. I find it interesting that sometimes animals are not aware of the predator and prey mentality when it comes to making friends. Additionally, younger children find it easier to make friends among diverse nationalities. They don't know what it means to be a bigot. They couldn't tell you the meaning of prejudice. In both examples of humans and animals, the negative response is built into their nature. But there's something different about how they look upon diversity.

If you were to go into a kindergarten class and ask each child what makes them unique from their classmates, the response may surprise you. Although they would notice a difference of hair color, eye color, and skin color, they would most likely not mention ethnic or religious background. And yet we as adults have a tendency to define others by race or creed.

What is it that changes us from having that childlike perception to having a judgmental attitude? That answer can be found in our upbringing. What is it we heard or viewed as we were growing up? Were there racial slurs used in the household? Were we taught to believe that our church was the only right belief? How do we modify our behavior from so many years of wrong teaching? The answer to that question is in our thought process. Just as it's crucial to adjust how we see ourselves, it's even more important to transform our way of viewing everyone else.

I like to use the example of having a glass of water and pouring dirt into the glass. Quickly the once clear water becomes cloudy. If you continue to put more and more dirt into the glass—well, the water will become mud. But if you begin to pour clean water back into the glass, the dirt will eventually spill over the sides, and you'll have your clean water once again. Think of your soul as the glass and your thought process as either dirt or clean water. Your soul consists of your mind, will and emotions. What you fill yourself with can determine whether you're seeing through a murky glass or a crystal clear one.

One good step to a revised thought process is to learn how to control your words. My first reaction to someone challenging me is to use my mouth to defend myself. In the first years of our marriage, my poor husband was on the receiving end of many verbal darts. Not that he even deserved most of them, but I was going to have the last word no matter what he tried to say. Thankfully he didn't pay much attention to me when I was in that mode, and I learned just to keep my mouth shut, realizing there was no winner in a one-sided battle.

Because we were so familiar with one another's faults, it was easy to hit each other over the head with the word of God. Friends wondered how we ended up together, since it looked as if we were always arguing. One friend deemed us the "Bickersons." We soon learned to pray for each other, rather than try to change each other. Funny how we later found out that the things that irritated us the most were what we actually needed.

I've become more relaxed about admitting when he's right and I'm wrong. I don't always have to have the last word. I'm more aware of Greg's trigger points and when to walk away from an argument. The one thing I have grown to appreciate from him is when he says, "You're so cute when you're angry." How do you stay mad at that?

Your choice of delivery of anything said can change the meaning of the words spoken. A simple change in tone can make the receiver hear a completely different message than intended. An example would be when the pastor of a church begins to talk about giving. A pleading tone can give the impression of desperation requiring the listener to feel pity with a tendency toward guilt. However, a grateful tone can lead the giver to a sense of compassion with an attitude of wanting to help the church.

It's interesting that now, in the age of social media, we feel more comfortable writing our words than speaking them. This gives the writer a way to hide behind the words. There are things said that would never be spoken face-to-face. Rejection can be easily conveyed if there is little chance for immediate retribution. Unfortunately, the written word can sometimes be mistaken if the reader has a flawed mindset while trying to interpret the message. It always makes me laugh when someone sends an email with all capital letters to indicate they're angry or trying to make a point. HOW IRRITATING!

Whether by the spoken or written word, we convey what's really deep down in our hearts. "From out of the heart, the mouth speaks." (Luke 6:45) You can't always hide your motivation from people. Some may not quite understand what you're trying to say, but others can discern your intent just by listening to how you say something.

I have repeated the same theme of what a difference it makes when we consider our words and the attitude behind them. Maybe because of how important a kind word is to people. No matter what your past made you feel, there is never an excuse for treating others badly. Consider behaving the way you would want them to act toward you. Nothing bad can come from a good deed or word. It will change the way you see yourself as well.

I disagree with the old saying, "sticks and stones may break my bones, but names will never hurt me." Words can be incredibly damaging. Bruises on the outside will one day heal. But internal scars can be forever. We must learn how to pour more of the pure water into us in order to get rid of all the dirt that was given to us.

CHAPTER 6

Art of Perfection

No one is perfect—not one! However, there are some who do claim to be perfect. We'll just leave that as our secret and not tell them. But what does it mean to be perfect? Is it something that was communicated by others who decided that we should be perfect? Is it an emotion that was developed within us as a defense mechanism to protect us from negative experiences? Or is it an attitude that we believe about ourselves because of great intelligence or incredible talents?

Ironically, the word perfect does not always mean without fault. It can also mean to be complete or whole. The Bible talks about David who had a "perfect heart toward God." But if you read about David's life you'll find there was nothing perfect about the human David. What was perfect was that he was entirely or completely given over to loving God.

Did he ever sin? Of course he did. He did things that you and I in this lifetime would never consider. But he did repent and move on in his life to serving his Lord God. In no time of David's life did he ever act as if he was perfect. But he did desire to do the right thing before God. His perfection was a righteousness that only God understood.

Righteousness does not come just by reading the Word of God or by taking place in church rituals. It doesn't come by knowledge alone or your kind actions. It is not a trait that is easily attained by expressing your belief in God. It is only produced by fire!

We are tried by that fire and anything that is not right is burned in that same fire. Fire is tribulation and tribulation produces patience. Patience produces character and that character becomes hope. A hope that says God loves you and He will continue to mold you into that upright individual you always wanted to become.

There's a difference between doing good and being good. Many times I have heard people who think what they do in life is good enough for them to make it into heaven. But what I understand is that you need to have a mindset of always wanting to please God. This means diving deep inside your heart and dealing with the issues that cause you to do the wrong thing. By *heart* I don't mean the organ that pumps your blood. I'm talking about the part of you that houses your thoughts and emotions. It's much easier to write a check for the poor than it is to deal with a way of thinking about them.

We don't need to tell anyone about what we think. We just need to take everything to God in prayer and repentance. I realize from experience that it is not always easy to consider every bad thought or fantasy. But this is why we're told to bring every thought captive. That means we should be constantly vigilant about what we think and how we move on that thought.

Do you have to work under unfair management? Do you have issues with unloving family members? How do you handle your emotions when the first response is to be negative? When the thought of retaliation begins, you should stop and first consider the individual's reason for treating you badly.

There's no excuse for someone abusing you. But to strike back at them would only make the situation worse. What if your reaction would be to pray and ask God to help them? Not only does that work for your good, but that also works for their good. How great would it be if everyone had that same response? This is not to say that you can't stand up for yourself. No one should be a victim.

I grew up understanding what it meant to be a victim. My mother was abused by my father, both emotionally and physically. She didn't have the strength to leave, but I longed for the day when I was old enough to leave home.

I am the oldest of four and my relationship with dad was not always hard. When I was a little girl, dad took me to his club where I learned to play pool and shuffle board. He sometimes took me along to high school football games where I stood proudly at the end zone with his friends. Knowing what my dad did for a living was like being in a mob movie but without the shootings. I thought it was cool and I looked up to him. I wanted to be just as tough and above the law as he was.

Mom told me about a time when I decided I didn't want to go to bed. They left me in the living room and quietly observed me. She said I sat in dad's chair and reached for his cigarettes. I packed them down like he did and took one out, putting it in my mouth. Then I grabbed his coffee cup and sat there acting like I was in charge. That lasted until the stark realization that it was dark and I was alone. She thinks I was just about three years old. I started my revolution very young.

Later in my teens dad and I fought, a lot. Sometimes it was just verbal attacks but too many times it was physical. I remember the last one we had, I kicked him hard and he never touched me again. Rather than fight me, he resorted to packing my clothing and throwing me out of the house.

I lived with my aunt and uncle for about a month. They were just starting a family and I couldn't help financially. I'll always be grateful to them for opening up their home. Then I stayed overnight with two girls I barely knew and just for one night. I slept on a mattress in their attic. Except for a small square window it was very dark and thankfully, I couldn't see what I was sharing the space with. Then I went to a friend shortly after she was married and her new husband let me stay with them. Her parents were not very happy about that, so I moved back home. Eventually, I found a new friend and room mate. Mom was devastated. She cried and said she would go into my old room just to smell my perfume. Her first born had finally fled the coop.

After I was able to forgive him, my relationship with dad changed. I was no longer in his control and it was easier for me to see both my parents in a different light. They were people too and they had their own issues to deal with. Things had settled down after we were all grown and out of the house. I actually enjoyed visiting them. It was like meeting my mom and dad for the first time.

Do not let anyone tell you who or what you are and then believe it for yourself. Unfortunately, you can't stop someone from saying nasty things to you. But you can stop yourself from believing in what they say. People who are insecure are that way because they decided to wear the cloak of a lie. Someone once told them that they couldn't do or would never become anything. They listened, believed and took ownership of whatever they were told. If that is you – get rid of that covering. Shake it off and put on a new one that only you have possession of. Confess to yourself that God has created you and He loves His own creation. You are special and unique!

My husband has been told he has a quiet confidence about him. Maybe that's because he doesn't always respond to rejection in a negative way. No, he is not perfect. However, he does look for ways to work through the contention with a more positive approach. I have witnessed few times when he reacted by becoming very annoyed. And in those times, I believed he had every right to respond defensively. I even told him that I thought he needed to be more outraged for what was coming at him. His response to me was to pray. Does that make him weak? No, just the opposite; it's more difficult to walk away from a fight than to stay.

I've learned a great deal from him and his reactions to conflict. I was once a person who would actually look for a reason to argue. I now know that came from a latent hostility that was brewing within me for years. We learned to use our words as weapons, since as young children we couldn't physically challenge the abuser. I became quite defensive. I was going to be the victor no matter what the controversy. How did that work for me?

Not well, considering I not only lost many conflicts, but I also became a very angry person. I didn't realize what I'd become until a former classmate said she was afraid of me in school. That was a shock, since I thought I was a nice girl. It set me back enough to look into my past. I often attracted the wrong type of relationship. Looking for the negative makes you ill both inside and outside.

Thankfully, God saw the part of me that wanted to do what was right. I just needed a shove in that direction. I want the best for others as well as myself. It took some time for me to first admit my wrongs. Now it's become an every-day process for me to look at my motives. Don't be afraid to say you're sorry to someone. It's the most healing process you can experience. Let God change you. It doesn't hurt or take away from who you are. The rewards are so much greater than the actual sacrifice.

Every morning, you wake up to a new day—an awe-some opportunity for making a difference. Choice can be the greatest gift anyone can receive, a gift given by our Creator. When someone tells me they don't believe in God, I have to ask why. So often people say they have a hard time believing in a god that would allow children to starve to death or that a loving god would not cause so much suffering in the world. The fact is that God does not want anyone to suffer. But what He does want is for everyone to have the freedom of choice. Unfortunately, that freedom becomes bondage when we choose to do what is wrong. Making the right decision is not always easy. Before you do anything, stop to think of the end result. Who does it affect, and what is the long term outcome?

I don't live in fairytale land, and I'm not always whistling a happy tune. No one gets on my nerves more than me! I do have bad days, and, yes, I get angry. I have learned to step back and review the whys and hows of my feelings. Sometimes this is not my first reaction, but I've been getting better at stopping the emotional roller coaster.

We often make excuses for our bad behavior. Stop saying you're a product of your environment. Stop blaming others for the way you respond to negative experiences. If your parents were abusive, you don't have to be abusive. If your dad was an alcoholic, you don't need to be an alcoholic. If your mom was depressed, you don't have to be depressed.

We continue to walk in the footprints of those we once followed after. But if those footprints lead you to a destructive lifestyle, then start making a new path. Begin your day by first speaking positively about yourself. Change what you say, then change what you do. Be the first one in your family to blaze a new trail of optimism.

CHAPTER 7

What Really Hurts?

I have two beautiful step-daughters and each of them created four equally beautiful and talented children. There was only one time when all eight of them were gathered together at our house. Treasure your children and grand children while you have them close. Consider each minute you spend with them a blessing. Even the most annoying moments were so much more enjoyable then not having them around. Time goes by all too quickly. I have pictures from that day and will always consider it one of my best days ever.

When our grandchildren were small, my husband and I had the pleasure of babysitting on some weekends. They loved to play in our large backyard where we had a pond with a fountain running near a small bridge that crossed the water. Our deck was wood, and some areas had small splinters sticking up. We warned the kids not to run in bare feet. Inevitably, one of them would run into the house crying. We would clean the cut, put on a Band-Aid, and give the I-told-you-so speech.

Our youngest granddaughter was so upset when she saw the blood on her foot that she began to scream in terror. I told her not to worry, that her foot was just leaking. She asked what that meant, and I explained that we had fluid inside of us. I told her that when a cut happened anywhere on our body, that fluid would leak out. That was enough explanation for her that the crying stopped, and she went on playing with her siblings. Funny how quickly our fears are calmed when we recognize the mountain we saw is only a small molehill.

As a worship leader for over twenty years, I tried not to take the expressions of the congregation personally. However as an artist, I was still looking for recognition from someone in the crowd. One day a newcomer to our church was standing in plain sight. After a few songs, I noticed she made a face that I could only believe was of disapproval. Soon she looked away and hung her head as if to say, "This music is awful." Immediately I began the process of self-doubt and couldn't wait for the session to end.

Later that day, I ran into her in the lady's room. She could not have been nicer and expressed to me her gratitude for the songs that we chose. She said that the words were speaking to her and that she was dealing with some personal conviction. The songs made her cry. After thanking her for the kind words, I began some internal retrospection of my own. What is it about us that just a look or a bit of body language can cause us to question our own decisions? How much of our life choices have been made due to other's reactions.

Can you count grains of sand or stars in the sky, or compare each snowflake? Of course not, and yet we continue to believe that we need to look or act like everyone else. You are a unique individual, separate and different from the rest. Magazine covers, movies, television shows all put us into a "fantasy reality." You may never look like a model, sing like a bird, or become the next great inventor. But what you can do is help to change the world in your small part of it.

First, stop believing the lies about yourself. You don't need to develop a thick skin. Just develop a new attitude toward the negative. When people tell me not to take it personally, I have to laugh. It is personal when you're rejected, but the way you react to it is what matters the most. Good things happen to bad people, and bad things happen to good people. Remember, it rains on the just and the unjust. That's life. The only difference between the good and the bad is how they respond.

If you get angry, get angry. Just do it with control. Learn how to discern when someone is being nasty to you and why. What is it that they're going through that day? Is it really you they're mad at, or is it something else they're trying to deal with in their own lives. Stand up for yourself and speak the "truth in love." (Ephesians 4:15)

Walk away from a volatile situation, and think before you act. It's so much easier to seek revenge than it is to consider why the person is hurting you. What is it about what they said that cuts you so deeply? Maybe that rejection is closely related to how you really feel about yourself.

Spend more time by trying to help others. When you take your eyes off you, there's so much more to see around you. Make sympathy and compassion your best friends.

Ignore self-pity and depression. They kill and destroy. You're so much stronger than that.

You can't win the war if you don't know you're in a battle. So begin your day by loving you. The strong, confident person is not so easily swayed by the lies of an enemy. Once you prepare yourself by focusing on the positive, every dart that comes will be deflected by your own self-assurance.

Finally, treat others with the same respect you want. Keep your words under control and your thoughts in line. Negative people are magnets for rejection. This is where faith comes into play. You must begin believing without seeing. You're not alone. God wants the absolute best for you.

It's not that He's a tough task master and enjoys watching you reap what you sow; it's that God is Spirit, and when you remove yourself from His will by doing wrong, you put yourself in harms way. Yes, He says He will never leave you or forsake you. However, as in any promise there are stipulations. He can't protect or help when you're in total rebellion.

Not sure if you're wrong or in rebellion? Do a thought process check. What does your conscience tell you? What does your lifestyle tell you? Do you apologize or compromise what you believe in because you're afraid of man? Stop complaining; speak positively even if your current circumstances don't look positive. Next time you feel depressed because you weren't accepted, remember that Jesus Christ Himself was rarely accepted, and He is God!

Everything I've shared with you is not a life that I consider to be sad or depressing. I feel quite the opposite. If I can look back at anything, I would have to say that even the negative experiences were ones where I learned a great deal. It may not feel to you now that what you're going through is something you can learn from, but trust me when I say that years from now you'll recognize the lesson.

Even when the cruelty is not your fault, there's still a way to move forward from the past. Don't hold onto it. Cry just enough to let it out, be angry just enough to do something about it, and stress just enough to find a solution. Most importantly, pray, and ask God to show you a way out. He is faithful!

When you were in school and you didn't understand the subject, you asked questions. When you got a new job and had to go through training, you asked a lot of questions. So why wouldn't you come before the Creator of all things and ask questions?

Talk to God as if He were right there and don't worry about how you pray, just talk to Him.

Even when I was young and acted as if I knew it all, I still asked God why. Be warned that sometimes your answer may not be what you want to hear and might take longer than you care to wait. Either way, you will receive a response.

In first grade I would move over on my seat to give my angel room. Soon after that my angel would be too busy to sit. The doctor told my parents that I had leukemia at a very young age. Later blood tests confirmed only a strain of mono. I fell off a very high sliding board when I was a little girl and hit my head. I was thrown into a radiator by accident and again hit my head. I was hit by a car when riding my bike when I was 12. Neighbors watched as

I was tossed into the air landing on the opposite side of the street, again on my head. Thankfully, no other cars were coming on that normally very busy road. That same year I was hospitalized with a paralyzed portion of my face that went away within a month. I did a lot of things as a teenager that by all accounts should have put me in the hospital or worse, the morgue. My husband said that when we met my angel asked his angel to trade. Whatever the reason, God only knows, my life was spared.

I refer to my teenage years as the "dark years". From starting to smoke cigarettes at thirteen, drinking at age fourteen, drugs at fifteen and so on. But there were two disturbing events that almost destroyed me. At the time I thought I could do whatever I wanted without fear of consequence. Two weeks after I turned eighteen I made the second worse decision of my life.

While a group of us were hanging out, I was approached by a guy asking if I knew anyone that had some hash to sell. I knew a number of dealers and was quite smitten by one. We had been seeing one another for sometime and I asked him if I could take care of the deal, just to make a little money on the side.

He was not very enthused with the idea and was worried that it was not safe for me. I assured him that I knew the buyers and everything was going to be okay. Little did I know that it was a set up for local drug dealers and there I was, unaware of my arrogance. That night I got into a car in the back seat with two men in the front. They asked me how much I had and what it cost. They did me a favor by only purchasing half of what I had. Later I found out that act of kindness kept me from a long prison sentence.

Four months later, my father called me at work to say there were two detectives at our home to arrest me. Fortunately for me, my father knew both of them and they allowed him to bring me in rather than take me out in hand cuffs at my workplace. The next few months were terrifying. It was to my advantage that it was a first time offence. If I had the chance now, I would thank them for eventually "scaring me straight".

The first horrible decision I made was not having my baby at the age of nineteen. Just a year prior to becoming pregnant myself, I tried to talk a friend out of having an abortion. I was so against the idea, until it happened to me. I was afraid of raising a child on my own especially when the father didn't believe it was his. What kind of mother would I become on drugs and drinking every night. What kind of example would I be to a little one that needed me to be mature and not a party girl?

That choice made me think a lot about my so called convictions. Apparently, they weren't that solid and being weak made me angry. My life up to this point had been based on doing whatever made me feel good and not thinking of others. I damaged my reputation, embarrassed my family and lived with a guilt I couldn't shake.

One night at a party where most of us were high on LSD, I watched a guy fall over and begin to have a seizure. I was told this happened to him regularly when he drank. Not knowing what to do or if I could help, I stood there in fear. It was then that I saw myself as a completely different person and I didn't like her at all.

Before that night I never thought I would be so far removed from reality that I couldn't help someone in need. That night I seriously began to consider my lifestyle. I started to ask the God that I knew as a child to help me change. It was one of those times when you make deals with God. I asked Him to give me the ability to stop doing drugs and I promised to become more of what he wanted from me. Change didn't happen overnight. I spent days considering who I was and who I should be. There were times when I questioned everything and everyone I was around. It was no one else's fault. It was my responsibility and my life. But every time I looked in the mirror, I wasn't sure who I was seeing. Insecurity, doubt, fear, and rebellion had become my friends. I knew deep down inside that was not who I wanted to be.

Finally, at the age of twenty, I decided to stop destroying myself. A dear friend at work had invited me to go to a youth meeting at his church. I saw young people reading the Bible and praising the God that I had walked away from years ago. I made the decision to turn around and walk back into His arms again. I was led to pray a prayer of repentance and ask Jesus Christ into my heart. When I left the meeting, I was no longer the same person.

I started to see myself and others differently. I began a war against the negative in my past and got rid of the demons that kept me bound. I started over again in a more positive light. My thoughts, words and actions changed over the years. No longer did I want to live in rebellion. It has been a fight, but a good one.

It's now over thirty years later and I'm still in school learning about myself. I'm happy to say that I will never tire of the lessons. It tells me that God loves me enough to continue that good work. I still enjoy meeting new people, and, despite the tribulations I face, I still love life. I look forward to the day when I can see the whole person that *I was originally created to be!*

...greater is He that is in you, than he that is in the world. (I John 4:4)

I can do all things through Christ who gives me strength. (Philippians 4:13)

God has not given us a spirit of fear; but of power, and of love and of a sound mind.
(2 Timothy 1:7)

www.ingramcontent.com/pod-product-compliance
Lightning Source LLC
Chambersburg PA
CBHW071640050426
42443CB00026B/795